THE Passover Story

Anita Ganeri

Illustrated by
Rachael Phillips

Contents

A very long time ago, the Jews lived in Egypt. For a while, their lives were happy. But when a new Pharaoh came to the throne, things changed for the worse. He was afraid that the Jews would take over his land so he treated them as slaves, and set them to work building his royal cities.

It was back-breaking work, from dawn to dusk, but the worse things got, the stronger it made the Jews. So, one day, the Pharaoh gave a command.

"Take every Jewish new-born baby boy you can find," he told his soldiers, "and throw them into the river to drown."

At about this time, a Jewish woman had a baby boy. To hide him from the soldiers, she made a basket from bulrushes, covered it with tar to make it watertight, and placed the baby in it. Then she hid the basket among the reeds by the river.

Later that day, the Pharaoh's daughter came to bathe in the river. She spotted the basket and sent her maid to fetch it. When she opened the basket, she could not believe her eyes. Inside the basket was a baby and he was crying. The Pharaoh's daughter adopted the boy and brought him up as her own son in the royal palace. She called him Moses, which means 'drawn out', because she had drawn him out of the water.

Moses grew up as an Egyptian prince but he never forgot his Jewish family. One day, he saw an Egyptian cruelly beating a Jewish slave.

Moses was so angry, he killed the Egyptian and buried his body in the desert. When the Pharaoh found out, he was furious and ordered Moses to be put to death.

But Moses ran away to the land of Midian where he worked as a shepherd. One day, an extraordinary thing happened. Before Moses' eyes, a bush suddenly burst into flames but the bush didn't burn. Then Moses heard God's voice calling him.

"Moses!" God said. "I have seen how much my people are suffering in Egypt and have come to save them. Go to the Pharaoh and tell him to set the Jews free. Then lead them out of Egypt to freedom."

Moses returned to Egypt, as God had commanded, and asked the Pharaoh to let the Jews go. But the Pharaoh refused and made the Jews work harder than ever. Again and again, Moses asked for their freedom but the Pharaoh would not listen. So God sent ten terrible plagues to punish the Pharaoh and the Egyptians.

First, the River Nile turned into blood. Then there were plagues of frogs, lice and wild beasts. Next, a horrible disease killed the Egyptians' cattle, then people suffered from painful boils. Storms flattened their fields and locusts ate their crops. Then it was as dark as night for three days. Even after all this, still nothing would change the Pharaoh's mind.

The tenth plague was the most terrible of all. The first-born son in every Egyptian family died. Before he sent this last plague, God told the Jews to cook a meal of roast lamb and to be ready to leave their homes. They did not have time to bake proper bread so they made thin, flat bread which did not rise. While they ate their meal of lamb and bread, the angel of death passed over the Jewish houses and left them alone. Only Egyptian children were killed.

After this plague, the Pharaoh finally called Moses to him. "Take your people and leave Egypt," he said. "I do not want any more of your dreadful plagues. Your people are free."

So the Jews quickly gathered their belongings, and followed Moses out of Egypt into the desert. God sent a cloud to show them the way by day, and a fire to guide them by night.

But when the Pharaoh heard that the Jews had escaped, he changed his mind again and sent his soldiers to bring them back to Egypt.

The Jews were trapped. Before them lay a lake called the Sea of Reeds; behind them thundered the Egyptian war-chariots. But God came to their rescue. He sent a wind which parted the waters so that the Jews could cross the dry lake bed safely. Then the waters roared back again, and drowned the Egyptian soldiers as they tried to follow the Jews.

Some months after leaving Egypt, the Jews reached Mount Sinai. Their journey had been long and hard, and they were tired and frightened. While they pitched camp, Moses climbed to the mountain top to pray to God.

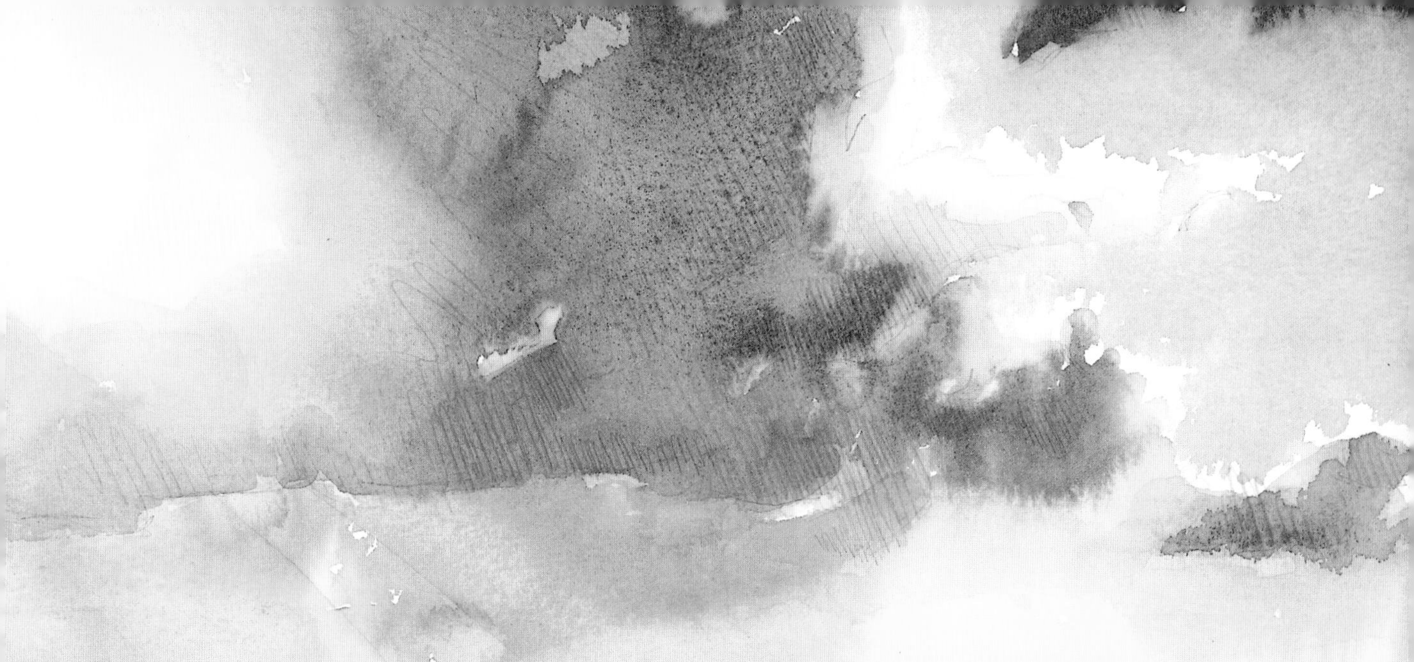

"Go back to your people and tell them this," God told Moses. "If they obey me, they will be my special people."

Three days later, God called Moses to the top of the mountain again. There he gave Moses ten commandments for the Jews to follow. He wrote the commandments on tablets of stone and told Moses to teach them to his people.

Then, for forty more days and forty nights, the Jews wandered through the desert, carrying God's laws with them, until, after many problems and difficulties, God led them safely to the land of Israel, their Promised Land.

Passover Celebrations

In March or April, Jews remember their ancestors' escape from Egypt with the festival of Passover (or Pesach in Hebrew). In preparation for Passover, the whole house is cleaned to get rid of any trace of hametz. This means bread, biscuits and cakes that contain yeast to make them rise. A candle is used to hunt out hametz and a feather to brush up any crumbs. At Passover, Jews do not eat hametz but remember the thin, flat bread their ancestors made by eating only matza, which is made of just flour and water, without yeast.

A Special Meal

The most important part of the Passover celebrations is a meal called the Seder meal. Each dish has a special meaning. For example, horseradish is a bitter food. It reminds the Jews of how unhappy their ancestors were in Egypt. The egg and lamb bone are offerings to God. The green vegetable, such as lettuce or parsley, is a sign of spring and new life.

A Passover Recipe

At Passover, Jewish people eat many special foods. Part of the Seder meal is a sweet dish called charoset. It reminds Jews of the cement or mortar their ancestors used to make buildings for their Egyptian masters. Try following this recipe and making your own charoset.

ASK AN ADULT TO HELP YOU

Ingredients:

4 eating apples
1 cup of mixed nuts
1 cup of raisins or sultanas
4 tablespoons of grape juice
1 level teaspoon of cinnamon

What to do:

1. Peel and core the apples. Chop them into small pieces or grate them finely.
2. Chop the nuts. You can do this by putting them in a plastic bag and crushing them with a rolling pin.
3. Mix the apples, the nuts and all the other ingredients together.

A Song for Passover

After the Seder meal, Jewish people sing a song called the Dayennu. In Hebrew, Dayennu means 'it would have been enough'. The song thanks God for all the good things he did for the Jewish people's ancestors after they escaped from Egypt. Here are a few verses from the song:

Had He brought us out of Egypt,
And not fed us in the desert,
Brought us out of Egypt,
Well then - Dayennu!

Had He brought us to Mount Sinai,
And not given us the Torah,
Brought us to Mount Sinai,
Well then, Dayennu!

Had He given us the Torah,
And not led us into Israel,
Given us the Torah,
Well then - Dayennu!

Had He led us into Israel,
And not given us the prophets,
Led us into Israel,
Well then - Dayennu!

If you enjoyed this book,
why not read another book in this series?

The Christmas Story (hbk)	0 237 52473 2
The Christmas Story (pbk)	0 237 52468 6
The Christmas Story Big Book	0 237 52359 0
The Easter Story (hbk)	0 237 52531 3
The Easter Story (pbk)	0 237 52475 9
The Easter Story Big Book	0 237 52470 8
The Hanukkah Story (pbk)	0 237 52653 0
The Hanukkah Story Big Book	0 237 52652 2
The Divali Story (pbk)	0 237 52471 6
The Divali Story Big Book	0 237 52469 4